Steam Memories: 1950's – 1960's

No. 108: BR Locomotive W... Scottish Region

David Dunn

Copyright Book Law Publications 2019
ISBN 978-1-909625-46-4

INTRODUCTION

When British Railways was created on 1st January 1948 Scotland could boast no less than five workshops which were all active overhauling and repairing steam locomotives which served what became known as the Scottish Region. Twenty years later when steam motive power was finally eliminated from BR's metals, the ScR only had one locomotive workshop. During those twenty years from Nationalisation to the end of steam on BR dozens of locomotive works throughout the country had succumbed to what was termed as rationalisation.

Scotland's five establishments were 'rationalised' gently at first with Kilmarnock losing locomotive repairs in 1952 and then concentrating on the scrapping of redundant steam locomotives before the cessation of that facility in July 1959. The former Highland works at Lochgorm ceased locomotive repairs in the early 1960s so that the premises could be adapted for diesel locomotive servicing, and repair. Inverurie which was amongst the last to handle steam motive power went through a very short transition with a view to handling diesels but alas the works was closed before the 1960s passed into another decade. The last two workshops were located, appropriately perhaps, in the heart of Glasgow where the former North British Railway shops had been chosen to look after some of the last steam repairs on BR. When the last locomotive left the workshops at Cowlairs the range of buildings forming the locomotive, carriage, and wagon shops were demolished in 1968. That event left one more workshop to overhaul, maintain and repair the diesel locomotive fleet north of the border; the refurbished St Rollox works of the erstwhile Caledonian Railway had survived to pass into a new era under British Rail.

As usual albums such as this can only be put together with the help of numerous people who unselfishly allow us to use their historic images. Amongst the organisations regularly supporting us is the Armstrong Railway Photographic Trust (ARPT) and to which we give our thanks. A number of individuals have also given us access to their collections and we would like to express our thanks to: George Ives, Bill Reed, Stuart Ashworth, the late Ian Falcus, Howard Forster, the late Paul Claxton, W. Stuart Sellar, Michael Halbert and the late EE (Teddy) Smith.

David Dunn, Cramlington, January 2019.

(Cover):   See Page 7.

(Title page):   **The works shunter at St Rollox, ex-Caley 'Pug' No.56025 earns a living pottering around the shops in September 1957.** *L. Turnbull (ARPT).*

Printed and bound by The Amadeus Press, Cleckheaton, West Yorkshire
First published in the United Kingdom by Book Law Publications, 382 Carlton Hill, Nottingham, NG4 1JA

COWLAIRS

V2 No.60836 inside Cowlairs in 1966; stripped of its motion and uncoupled from its tender, was this the time when it was decided to condemn the 2-6-2? This works visit is not even entered on the Engine History Card or any other similar official document so we know nothing of the time period No.60836 spent in the works or why. Condemned on the last day of 1966, the V2 was sold to a Motherwell scrapyard in July 1967. *D.R. Dunn collection (ARPT)*.

Cowlairs scrapyard 1st April 1964 with Hughes 'Crab' No.42830 being dismantled and cut up for scrap! With the tender down to the chassis, the cab and smokebox gone, the interesting bits of the boiler and firebox await. Stanier Cl.5 No.44801 is next in line. The scrapyard here polished-off a lot of steam locomotives during those momentous years of the 1960s when surprises were everywhere, especially in scrapyards. The trick was to be there when the surprise was there otherwise you would miss it and everyone else would have seen it, or more intriguingly the surprise arrived, was cut up without anybody recording its demise and therefor nobody knew a thing! In 1964 Cowlairs polished off an A3, four V2s, a 'Jubilee', three B1s, one J37, one J38, two 'Crabs', a pair of Peppercorn K1s, a 2P 4-4-0, a 4F 0-6-0, two 4P 2-6-4Ts. The previous year saw eight 'Jubilees' – all from English sheds – cut-up, the two ex–WR Pannier tanks which did service on the Dornoch branch were dealt with, and forty-odd others from V2s to Y9s and seemingly everything in between. *George Ives.*

The Erecting shop on 7th April 1957 with a selection of former LNER locomotives undergoing various levels of overhaul or repair; those identifiable include J38 No.65908, Y9 No.68097, and B1 No.61402. Starting with the 0-6-0, No.65908 was in shops for a Heavy Intermediate – 2nd April to 4th May 1957 – which was its penultimate visit to Cowlairs for shopping; after its October 1958 Light Intermediate, Inverurie took care of the Thornton Junction based J38's maintenance requirements. The Y9 was amongst the oldest in her class and had been built here in December 1887. At this shopping the 0-4-0ST was undergoing a Heavy Intermediate – 27th March to 20th April 1957 – during what also turned out to be the engine's penultimate visit to Cowlairs; its final visit to the workshops took place after it was condemned at St Margarets its home shed on 14th October the following year. The last visit to Cowlairs was for breaking up during September 1959. Now you might come to the conclusion that BR locomotive overhauls took on a seasonal trend because Dundee based B1 No.61402 was also in shops for a Heavy Intermediate – 22nd March to 20th April 1957 – only it's third shopping since being put into traffic 27th April 1950. The scene reveals a typical workload and customers for the period. *Bill Reed.*

Forward three years to May 1960 and some of the Scottish based BR Standards are requiring time in Cowlairs shops with two Class 4s, 76074 (Eastfield) and 76100 (Dawsholm) in varying state of undress but having a thorough seeing–to! No.76074 was one of the first sent to ScR arriving new in November 1956. It was now receiving a Heavy Intermediate overhaul – except for the cab side, it looks almost new in this image. No.76100 is getting similar treatment but this is certainly Cowlairs and not Doncaster shops. We are once again in the centre bay of Cowlairs Erecting shop's three erecting bays. Each bay had three roads with the middle road of each having access to the yard at the north end of the workshop building. Cowlairs became an operational workshop for the Edinburgh & Glasgow Railway in 1842 and remained under their ownership for twenty-three years until the E&GR became part of the North British Railway. Locomotives had been built here since 1844 but the last examples – the N15s – were constructed for the LNER in 1924; some 850 engines had been constructed during those eighty years. Thereafter only overhauls, repairs and scrapping took place but over the years up to closure in 1966 thousands of locomotives passed through the works. Besides the locomotive shops, carriage and wagon shops were also engaged on the site with the wagon shops standing alongside the western wall of the erecting shop, and beyond that, attached to the wagon shop's west wall was the carriage shop. It would be fair to say that the wagon shop was almost four times larger than the locomotive shop whereas the carriage shop was even bigger! Demolition of the 167 acre site by a contractor from Coatbridge started in 1968. *Stuart Ashworth collection.*

Staying in the centre bay, we go forward just one year this time to 20th May 1961. The midday sun is highlighting the three Standards on display, a boiler–less Cl.4 tank, a Cl.5, and particularly a Kingmoor 'Clan' No.72006 CLAN MACKENZIE which was receiving its second Heavy General overhaul, the first event having taken place at Crewe in January 1956. Cowlairs also carried out 'Generals' on sisters Nos.72000, 72002, 72004, 72005, 72007, 72009. The remaining members of the class – 72001, 72003, 72008 – received Heavy Intermediate overhauls at Cowlairs but their first and only 'Generals' were carried out at St Rollox. A visit to Cowlairs on Thursday 21st April 1960 found that BR Standards had virtually taken over the works with the following locomotives in and around the shops: two BR Std. Cl.6 4-6-2; eight BR Std. Cl.5 4-6-0; one BR Std. Cl.4 2-6-0; two BR Std. Cl.3 2-6-0; four BR Std. Cl.4 2-6-4T; two WD 2-10-0; four WD 2-8-0; three B1; two J39; two K2 withdrawn; one K3; one Diesel-Hydraulic 0-4-0 shunter. On the day when this image was recorded, two other 'Clans' were in shops: 72001 and 72005. Clan fact: 72003 CLAN FRASER went to meet her maker still carrying the early BR emblem the only Pacific so treated apart from accident damaged 46202 PRINCESS ANNE. *Stuart Ashworth collection.*

J72 No.68709 was the works shunter on 9th June 1957. One of the older members of the class, this J72 started work in November 1914 at Shildon as NER No.2192. It came to Eastfield, via Darlington, on 11th February 1939 where jobs such as this became its usual diet. When diesel shunters took over the works pilot job in 1958, No.68709 transferred to Kipps. From there it was downhill all the way going to Polmadie on 22nd March 1961 then Hamilton a month later. It was condemned on 26th February 1962 and sold for scrap some five months afterwards. In one of those tactical moves that BR used to perform regularly, this 0-6-0T didn't visit Cowlairs for overhauls after 1949 – it had received a General at Cowlairs in 1948 and an unknown repair in June 1949 but from thereon it had to go to Inverurie for attention. In 1951 it went to Aberdeenshire for a Heavy Intermediate, then, from 26th January to 4th March 1955, it was given a General and a replacement boiler. Note the NBR style shunters' step and grab handle. *W.S. Sellar.*

No this is not a newspaper stunt as was once performed on an ex–Midland Compound with Gorton works colluding to make a right 'pigs-ear' out of a 4-4-0 designated to haul a special excursion from Manchester to Blackpool. This is former North British Railway Class K 4-4-0 No.256 in undercoat whilst undergoing restoration on 18th May 1959. In reality the D34 was still BR No.62469 GLEN DOUGLAS but it would never wear that number again and would be withdrawn at No.256 on 19th October 1959. From that day on it was to be TLC, museums, and special workings. The 4-4-0 is stabled alongside what was the engine shed at Cowlairs in BR days and the road it is stabling on would take it into the steaming shed for tests. No.62469 spent three months inside Cowlairs being made ready for its new life and it was finally renumbered N.B.R. 256 on 24th July 1959. Whilst the 4-4-0 was operating special trains it was allocated to Dawsholm shed but on 17th December 1962 it was withdrawn once again to be lodged in a museum. Note the specially fitted wing plates at the front of the smokebox to lend some authenticity to the restoration. *F.W. Hampson (ARPT)*.

Here's one we fixed earlier! Thornton Junction's N15 No.69143, complete with the new BR crest, looks resplendent in the works yard on 9th June 1957 after completing a 'General' – 16th May to 8th June 1957. The overhaul was the engine's last before it was condemned 16th September 1960. But that's three years away and a lot of work and dirt – not to mention a transfer to Motherwell on the last day of November 1959 – will be plied on the N15 before then. Note the Junction or even the abbreviated version was dropped by the sign writers in the paint shop! No.69143 was taken to Inverurie for cutting up in October 1960. *W.S. Sellar.*

Three F7s migrated to Scotland in 1931–2 but only two of them became BR property. This is one of the pair, No.7094 – 7093 was the other – in the works yard on 24th May 1949 looking decidedly jaded and missing a few vital components. Both of the Scottish Region F7s were condemned on the same day, 8th November 1948 at St Margarets depot and then hauled to Glasgow to meet their fate. Our subject was given a General overhaul at Cowlairs in early 1947 and was given back the boiler it went into shops with during 1942 – No.C1810 – refurbished of course! Surviving boilers were getting a bit thin on the ground by 1947 so Cowlairs refurbished C1811 off No.7094 and placed it on sister 7093 when she had a General in June/July 1947. In typical Cowlairs fashion neither of the F7s received fresh paint at their 1947 overhauls! For the record, the third F7 which didn't make 1948 was Carlisle Canal's No.7593 which was condemned 20th April 1943. That is D34 No.2473 GLEN SPEAN behind which had been condemned eleven days previously and was awaiting cutting up. *K.H. Cockerill (ARPT).*

J88 No.68345 was one of the works shunters on 20th March 1959 and is seen entering the premises at the south end near the station with the Iron Foundry on the left, behind the fence. From this aspect we can see the footbridge in the right background which led from the station platform to the office building. The 0-6-0T had been transferred to Eastfield on 30th August 1958 from Dunfermline but nobody at 65A had bothered to paint out the Dunfermline legend on the bufferbeam. Similarly they had not bothered to affix a 65A shed plate either. When this J88 was condemned at Kipps on 29th December 1962, she was the last of the class. The thirty-five J88 were all constructed at Cowlairs between 1904 and 1919 – our subject here dated from 1912. All of them reached Nationalisation and the first to be condemned was No.68341 prematurely in November 1954 after falling into Kirkcaldy harbour! Being a shunting engine a platform was fitted behind the cab footsteps and a grab rail was attached to the lower bunker – I'm sure the H&S brigade would have something to say about such practices if they were required nowadays. Note the lack of a drawhook on the dumb bufferbeam. Now, about that chimney! When allocated to Dunfermline, No.68345 was loaned out to Blairhall Colliery in March 1956 and it was during that time when the original chimney was damaged – goodness knows how. On return to Dunfermline they fabricated this somewhat austere-looking chimney and the little tank retained the piece until condemned. Like a lot of her sisters, No.68345 was appropriately cut up here at Cowlairs in July 1963 whereas others in the class were cut up at Kilmarnock, Inverurie, St Rollox, or in private yards. *W.S. Sellar.*

GLEN FRUIN also known as 2480 awaits shopping in the works yard in early December 1949 prior to entering for a Heavy Intermediate overhaul – 16th to 30th December 1949. The Eastfield based D34 would emerge as No.62480 complete with the new BR emblem; it never did get the 1957 crest as its final shopping was a Light Intermediate at Inverurie during the summer of 1955 when it was then allocated to Kittybrewster. But it would emerge looking the part for its BR career with the parsimonious 'lick of paint' applied by Cowlairs in those post–war days. Although not exactly illustrated to advantage, the gable-ends of the Erecting shops can be seen above the locomotives' chimney and dome cover. Whilst bringing your view to the rear of the tender we can see two tall chimneys which must have been those used by a pair of former C11 'Atlantic' boilers employed near the wagon shops Those two specimens were once part of the NBR C11 Atlantic boiler pool – possibly – but they may have been the two boilers built in 1928 as spares – Nos.1511 and 1512 – and which had three Ross-pop safety valves each; three boilers built in 1924 also had the triple Ross-pop layout. It would have made sense to have employed the youngest of the 'Atlantic' boilers which by the time the class was withdrawn were no more than ten years old and have probably done even less time in service. *S.C. Crook (ARPT)*.

13

Although it looks withdrawn, Motherwell based WD 2-10-0 No.90762 was simply awaiting works on 7th April 1957. Cowlairs looked after all the Austerity 2-10-0s even though they were all allocated to former LMS depots – if anyone knows the reason behind that decision then this compiler would like to know please! The 2-8-0 WD were scattered a little more evenly amongst the ScR sheds but they too became the responsibility of Cowlairs shops. During the period in the 1960s when St Rollox works ceased locomotive repairs from March 1964, Cowlairs took on the burden of looking after most of the Scotland based steam locomotives with Inverurie taking on its share. But besides the Scottish Region charges, Cowlairs also handled Stanier Class 5s and 8Fs from the London Midland Region, WD 2-8-0s from the Eastern Region and others which sneaked below the radar. You could always note an England based locomotive that had attended Cowlairs because they used to apply the name of the home depot of the engine in uppercase letters on the front bufferbeam. On Sunday 31st January 1965 the following were in and around Cowlairs: three Cl.4 2-6-4T; one BR Std. Cl.4 2-6-4T; four BR Std. Cl.5 4-6-0; one BR Std. Cl.4 2-6-0; one 'Crab' 2-6-0, withdrawn; two V2, withdrawn; one J38; and twenty–three Stanier Cl.5 4-6-0s of which nineteen were from the LM Region. Some statistics for 1965 concerning locomotives from English sheds – ER and LMR – saw ten Ivatt Cl.4s, ninety–six examples of Stanier Cl.5s, thirteen BR Std. Cl.5s, and a lot of others from engine sheds as far south as Willesden and then up to and including Carlisle Kingmoor. *Bill Reed.*

INVERURIE

Five locomotives wait their turn for overhaul outside the Erecting shop at Inverurie on Tuesday 12th April 1955. We are looking at the west wall of the main building with the machine and fitting shop nearest the camera. The lofty Erecting shop forms the backdrop for the line of entrants. This is the view which greeted visitors using the main entrance on Harlaw Road. For the record, the five engines in the line-up were D40 No.62275, K2 No.61792, J37 No.64540, D30 No.62426, and N2 No.69503. The first four represent a good cross section of the classes normally dealt with here but the N2 was a departure from the usual tank engines visiting these shops. The six-coupled tank was a actually a new acquisition of Ferryhill shed (10th June 1954 ex–Kipps) so it was logical to send it to Inverurie for shopping but sending it to Cowlairs would not have appeared out of the ordinary if that had been the case. However few N2s had been to Inverurie for overhauls beforehand and the only known examples are: Parkhead's No.69500 which had a Light Intermediate in November/December 1953; No.69514, also from Parkhead, was undergoing an L/I whilst our subject was actually awaiting entry to the Erecting shop. No.69503 arrived at the works on Friday 8th April and by the end of the following week it would be located in the Erecting shop receiving a Casual Heavy overhaul which kept it indoors until 28th May when it was sent to Kittybrewster for running–in. So, there you have it only three N2s had ever ventured to Inverurie shops and we have a picture of the last example – but *see* later. *Ian Falcus.*

In 1898 the Great North of Scotland Railway began building new workshops for the construction, overhaul and repair of their locomotive fleet with operations eventually starting in 1903. The original site at Kittybrewster was too small for expansion and so a 25–acre green field site at Inverurie, some fifteen miles north-west of the former workshops in Aberdeen was chosen. Besides the locomotive shops, carriage and wagons workshops were also constructed and these facilities were working by 1905.

Only ten locomotives were ever constructed at Inverurie and these became GNofSR classes F and V with the building taking place between 1906 and 1921 – a period of fifteen years which would equate to… let's not bother with the maths! Those engines became LNER Class D40 after Grouping and largely remained intact into the British Railways era.

Although closed by BR in 1969, the main erecting building does not survive today unlike the former Carriage and Wagon shops – now apparently a Category B Listed Building – are in use for other purposes not associated with railways. Shortly before closure of the locomotive works some figures were revealed in a Motion and Question listed in *Hansard* for Wednesday 18th December 1968 from Mr. James Davidson MP for Aberdeenshire, West, thus: The population of the Royal Burgh of Inverurie was 5,267 and the locomotive workshops employs 580 men, one in four of the insured population of Inverurie. Of these men 224 are skilled whilst 204 were semi-skilled. There were 100 salaried staff and the rest were unskilled including 40 apprentices. The only other manufacturing in the town is a small paper mill. He explained that without the locomotive works Inverurie would be a town without a heart, unless there was a successful transplant from somewhere else. In his speech the Member for Aberdeenshire, West imparted a number of useful facts which although describe the modern workshop, gives us an insight as to what was happening at Inverurie in the days up to closure. For instance he stated that '…at present the carriage shop was working at full capacity, with occasional pockets of overtime. The wagon shop was in the same position. There was a lack of locomotive work or more to the point a lack of locomotives to repair – the workshop went over to diesel repairs some time ago – so that steel wagons were being repaired in the locomotive shop, by amicable agreement between management and staff. The blacksmith's shop too was very busy and working overtime. New equipment was installed in 1964. The works had an unsurpassed record of good labour relations…'

A 100–ton capacity overhead travelling crane with two 50–ton hoists, and a further two 10–ton auxiliary hoists had been installed in 1955 over the centre bay of the erecting shop whilst 40–ton cranes are located over the other bays. Each crane is one–man operated even though two hoists are used to lift locomotives and tenders. The increase in lifting capacity enabled Inverurie to take in locomotives such as Stanier Class 5s and Type 2 diesel locomotives.

The number of locomotives receiving attention at Inverurie varied like any other workshops for any number of reasons but the numbers found on the following dates from January 1948 is worth perusal; the first figure is the total number of locomotives in the shops; the locomotive wheelbase followed by a total of that type present with the + indicating withdrawn engines too. Diesels were being accepted at Inverurie for repairs from 1960 and they are designated as – Main Line ML, Shunters SH, and Railbus RB. For a more detailed listing of individual locomotives, the reader should visit the *Shed Bash UK* website which lists hundreds of locations and thousands of dates:

Date	Total	Details
20/01/48	33 -	0-6-0 **16**; 4-6-0 **1+1W**; 0-6-0T **2**; 4-4-0 **4+7W**; 2-4-2T **1**; 0-4-4T **1W**.
02/05/48	35 -	0-6-0 **11+1W**; 4-6-0 **7+1W**; 0-6-0T **2**; 4-4-0 **5+6W**; 0-4-4T **1+1W**.
25/08/49	20 -	0-6-0 **12**; 4-6-0 **1**; 2-6-2 **1**; 0-6-0T **1**; 4-4-0 **3**; 2-4-2T **1**; 0-4-4T **1**.
31/08/50	24 -	0-6-0 **11+2W**; 4-6-0 **2**; 2-6-0 **1**; 0-6-0T **2**; 4-4-0 **3**; 2-4-2T **1**; 0-4-4T **2**.
12/09/51	20 -	0-6-0 **6+2W**; 4-6-0 **1**; 2-6-0 **1**; 0-6-0T **1**; 4-4-0 **2+2W**; 2-4-2T **2W**; 0-4-4T **3**.
02/06/53	31 -	0-6-0 **13**; 4-6-0 **5W**; 0-6-0T **1**; 4-4-0 **5+3W**; 0-4-4T **2+2W**.
29/09/53	36 -	0-6-0 **15**; 4-6-0 **6W**; 0-6-2T **1**; 0-6-0T **1**; 4-4-0 **8+4W**; 0-4-4T **1W**.
16/08/54	24 -	0-6-0 **15**; 0-6-2T **2**; 0-6-0T **1**; 4-4-0 **5**; 0-4-4T **1**.
28/09/55	29 -	0-6-0 **19+1W**; 4-4-0 **4**; 0-4-4T **4**; 0-4-2T **1**.
14/02/56	23 -	0-6-0 **14**; 0-6-0T **3**; 0-6-2T **1**; 4-4-0 **4**; 0-4-4T **1W**.
16/10/56	24 -	0-6-0 **15**; 4-6-0 **1**; 4-4-0 **7**; 0-4-4T **1**.
17/05/57	19 -	0-6-0 **11**; 0-6-0T **1**; 0-6-2T **1**; 4-4-0 **4**; 0-4-4T **2**.
10/12/57	18 -	0-6-0 **14**; 0-6-0T **2**; 4-4-0 **2**; 0-4-4T **1**.
27/05/58	17 -	0-6-0 **14+1W**; 4-4-0 **2**.
09/01/59	21 -	0-6-0 **13**; 0-6-0T **1**; 4-4-0 **6**; 0-4-4T **1W**.
05/09/59	19 -	0-6-0 **9+3W**; 2-6-0 **1W**; 0-6-2T **2W**; 4-4-0 **4W**.
04/01/60	15 -	0-6-0 **7+5W**; 4-6-0 **1**; 4-4-0 **1+1W**.
13.06/60	30 -	0-6-0 **14+1W**; 4-6-0 **2**; 4-4-0 **1**; 0-4-2T **2W**; ML **6**; SH **4**.
22/05/61	29 -	0-6-0 **14+1W**; 4-6-0 **1**; 2-6-0 **1**; 2-6-4T **1**; 0-6-2T **1W**; 4-4-0 **2W**; ML **4**; SH **4**.
28/09/61	29 -	0-6-0 **14+2W**; 4-6-0 **1**; 0-6-0T **1W**; 2-8-0 **1**; ML **5**; SH **3**; RB **2**.
17/02/62	15 -	0-6-0 **8+2W**; ML **4**; SH **1**; **28** various locomotives resident in scrapyard.
21/04/62	24 -	0-6-0 **16**; 4-6-0 **1**; ML **2**; SH **3**; **35** in scrapyard.
14/08/62	17 -	0-6-0 **6**; 4-6-0 **1**; ML **6**; SH **3**; **29** in scrapyard.
13/04/63	20 -	0-6-0 **4+11W**; ML **3**; SH **2**.
01/06/63	24 -	0-6-0 **4+4W**; 4-6-0 **2**; 2-6-4T **1**; 0-6-0T **1W**; 2-8-0 **2W**; ML **5**; SH **4**.
08-10 1963	17 -	0-6-0 **9**; 4-6-0 **4**; 2-6-0 **2**; 2-6-4T **2**.
10/08/65	29 -	0-6-0 **4+1W**; 4-6-2 **1**; 4-6-0 **3**; 2-6-0 **1**; ML **11**; SH **8**.

Fresh from the GE Lines of the Eastern Region! F4 No.67157 rests in the works yard in February 1948 less than a week after its transfer from Yarmouth Beach. The 2-4-2T had been summoned to north–east Scotland in order to work the Light railway from Fraserburgh to St Combs where fencing was minimal and livestock was left to roam over the tracks. In order to run on the branch cowcatchers were to be fitted at each end of the engine. That was the reason for (6)7157's visit to Inverurie on this date. It would be more than two years before the BR emblem and the 60,000 addition to its number was applied to this F4 and that too was done at Inverurie during a Light Intermediate overhaul in June 1950. Earlier we mentioned the workforce at Inverurie being good at what they did and an example of that remark can be related to No.67157's next shopping when on 30th June 1953 the F4 was taken into the shops for its first and only General overhaul at Inverurie. At such an event the boiler was taken off the locomotive and either replaced by another of the same Diagram or the original was repaired and put back onto the frames. The latter option usually meant that a locomotive was out of traffic for longer because boiler repairs were often slow affairs hence the normal replacement procedure. Obviously Inverurie didn't have a spare boiler and so the boiler which came off 67157 – No.2238 – was refurbished, renumbered to 26795 and put back. All of this was accomplished between the dates of Tuesday 30th June to Friday 17th July 1953 when No.67157 was returned to traffic – fifteen working days including two Saturday mornings. *A.R. Thompson collection (ARPT).*

13th November 1953! Yes, that is the date of this image. J37 No.64597 stands behind the D11/2 after receiving a Light Intermediate overhaul, with no painting this time except on the numberplate and 64A shed plate – 16th October to 13th November 1953 – and was ready to work home to St Margarets (allocated 26th October 1952 to 22nd April 1957). The dates have been inserted to try and bolster the evidence before you as ALLAN-BANE shows off its second LNER number 2692 in superb shaded transfers and with LNER, also in shaded transfers, on the tender! The smokebox carries the cast numberplate 62692. So, what was afoot some five years after the 'Director' should have lost its LNER number and identity? The official record has the D11/2 down as receiving a Casual Light repair at Haymarket shed (usually C/L repairs means patching up after accidents) on these dates but here we are at Inverurie. The truth behind the reason is stranger than fiction but it did happen and more than once to a number of locomotives. We do not have enough space here to tell the full story but look out for future publications to learn the truth. In the meantime, you can run a model of subject D11/2 on your layout and not be ridiculed! *S.C. Crook (ARPT).*

Thornton Junction's D30 No.62418 THE PIRATE is stripped in the Erecting shop in July 1955 ready for a General overhaul – 11th July to 17th August 1955. Note that head–dress is the order of the day; dirt, sparks, oils and grease were the enemy of the cranium hair and so measures were taken to try and keep the enemy at bay. There were three separate bays in the Erecting shop, one containing most of the boiler work, then locomotives, then locomotives and tenders. This was No.62418's first visit to Inverurie; another one during the summer of 1957 would see the D30 receive its final shopping and two years later it was condemned. *Brian Morrison.*

D40 No.62273 GEORGE DAVIDSON was the penultimate locomotive built at Inverurie during their on–off dalliance with locomotive construction from 1909 to 1921 when they managed to build just ten of these handsome 4-4-0s which all became members of LNER Class D40. The worksplate on the splasher below the nameplate simply states London & North Eastern Railway Inverurie 1921; the section where a number or figures should have been displayed in the centre of the plate was chiselled clear for some reason! Anyway, the date is sometime during October 1953 and the 4-4-0 had just completed a Light Intermediate overhaul – 28th September to 16th October 1953 – and is looking very smart too. Having spent all of its life – after it was put into traffic in June 1921 – working from Kittybrewster shed up to 18th February 1952, No.62273 transferred to Keith for its final three years before being condemned on 14th January 1955. This D40 ended its days as it had begun at Inverurie where it was dismantled on 26th February 1955. Now then, about the wall cladding at this place! From a distance, and indeed close-up too, some people could be forgiven for believing that the walls of the various workshops at Inverurie were constructed from concrete building blocks or even breeze blocks when in fact they were made from local granite. However, the bonding is not the prettiest I'm sure most would agree. *S.C. Crook (ARPT).*

Back to motive power! Being assessed, Perth's Pickersgill 4-4-0 No.54500 gets inspected prior to overhaul on Monday 22nd August 1960. The 3P was one of thirty–two engines – Nos.66 to 97 – introduced as late as 1920 during the Caledonian's last fling with four–coupled motive power. Very similar to the '713' and '918' classes from 1916, they weighed exactly the same at 61–tons 5–cwt but had cylinders which were just half an inch wider! However the LMS put them all in the same class; BR divided them on the cylinder issue. No.54500's Caledonian number was No.69. Anyway, the 4-4-0 passed its assessment and was taken into shops for overhaul which gave her another eighteen months working from Perth before withdrawal in March 1962. *C.J.B. Sanderson (ARPT)*

And this is what they look like with a bit of a clean and a coat of paint! Note also the lining which has been nicely applied by the Inverurie painters that on the footplate follows the curvature. The date is 23rd June 1957, a Sunday, and Dumfries based 3P No.54507 is ready for a spell of running–in – note the A (Aberdeen) 47 (duty) target already fitted – before working its way back to southern Scotland. The following morning should see steam raising, etc. taking place. J37 No.64547 behind has already done a week of tests after its Heavy Intermediate, and will be leaving the works shortly for its home shed at St Margarets. The older J37 would undergo a few more heavy overhauls over the next nine years and in March 1964 would transfer to Dundee Tay Bridge shed where it would before amongst the last steam locomotives working in Scotland. The ex–Caley 3P would not be so lucky and being essentially a passenger locomotive its services would not be required much after 1961 as diesel multiple units and Type 2 diesel locomotives took over the secondary passenger services once entrusted to it. No.54507 was withdrawn from Dumfries in December 1961 and later sold for scrap. *C.J.B. Sanderson (ARPT)*.

J37 No.64616 looks all the better for having received a Light Intermediate overhaul – 18th August to 7th September 1956 – complete with a coat of paint. The 0-6-0 will be on its way back to Thornton Junction shed within a few days good for another eighteen months of graft before another such overhaul in 1958. The engine is at the south end of the works site – where the sun shone all day – and behind is the south-east corner of the Erecting shop with the boiler house nearest the camera. *C.J.B. Sanderson (ARPT).*

August 1957 and J72 No.68750 has just completed a General overhaul – 2nd to 23rd August 1957 – which turned out to be its last. One of the Doncaster-built members of the class – Doncaster No.1631, to traffic 16th December 1925 – which was LNER number 566 until the general renumbering of 1946. Initially allocated to Sunderland, the 0-6-0T migrated to Kittybrewster in December 1934 and would have done a few stints here as works pilot just like sister No.68710 behind wearing the A18 target denoting working pilot. With its fortunes looking less than rosy, No.68750 was transferred to Polmadie on 3rd April 1961 and six weeks later it was on to Motherwell. In October 1961 Hamilton became the third ex–LMS shed in a row to use its services but it didn't end there because on 25th June 1962 the little 0-6-0T was sent to Dumfries where six months later she was withdrawn and sold almost immediately to a scrap yard in Shettleston! A couple of things of note applied by Inverurie include the 2F on the bunker side above the number (*see* next image), and the I 8-57 – denoting works and date of late overhaul – on the vertical edge of the running plate behind the bufferbeam. Oh yes, look at that crest! *C.J.B Sanderson (ARPT)*

J72 No.68710 was Inverurie works pilot – A 18 – on 23rd June 1957 and this Sunday evening image shows the six-coupled tank stabled over the pit which constituted the stabling point at this workshop. Many locomotive works had elaborate sheds for their fleet of pilots, others had makeshift shelters; Inverurie had this pit! We are in the south–east corner of the works site with the boiler house behind and the Erecting shop displaying its northlight – east-light more like – roof (the elaborate drainage system on the roof is quite something considering this is supposed to be the drier side of Scotland). Just like sister No.68750, our subject had used up all its works visits for overhauls and was now living on borrowed time but the pilot duties here would not be too arduous. Built at Darlington and coming into traffic in October 1920 as North Eastern Railway No.2303, the 0-6-0T went to Middlesbrough and was transferred to Keith on 15th March 1932 but three weeks later going to Kittybrewster shed from where it spent the rest of its life working duties such as this. Condemned 5th March 1959, No.68710 also went to Motherwell but to a rather large scrap yard located there. Note the 3FT on the cab sidesheet. This J72 was shopped eight months before No.68750. *C.J.B. Sanderson (ARPT).*

Tantalisingly hovering in the background of the previous image, N15 No.69186 shows off its robust lines on 23rd June 1957. Lining was still in force for the likes of this engine although it wasn't even fitted with vacuum brakes or screw couplings for working passenger trains! Heavy shunting and trip working was the lot of N15s such as this and No.69186 shows off the shunters grab handle but where was his foot board? The brackets are there but the timber plank has still to be fitted; perhaps that was a job for its home shed at St Margarets where the N15 spent the whole of its life. The 0-6-2T had just finished a Light Intermediate – 4th to 21st June 1957 – and was enjoying its first but not its last visit to Inverurie. The next time it required works it was condemned instead on 31st July 1959. Three months later on 13th October it was in the scrapyard at Inverurie being dismantled. Worthy of note the front splasher is yet to be lined and smokebox and shed plate need a coat of paint. *C.J.B. Sanderson (ARPT)*.

Kingmoor 'Crab' No.42832 looking extremely smart on a June morning in 1962. The types of locomotives visiting Inverurie during those final years was becoming more diverse as traditional workshops were either turning away their usual charges, or impending closure saw them winding down on admissions. This engine would normally have been dealt with at St Rollox or even Horwich but the refurbishment of the former Caledonian works meant its usual clientele had to go elsewhere. *Malcolm Foreman (ARPT).*

Towards the end of April 1954 and with the buds barely showing on the trees, Haymarket based D30 No.62437 ADAM WOODCOCK is receiving the finishing touches of a Heavy Intermediate overhaul – 5th to 30th April 1954 – and simmering in the yard whilst under steam. It would be interesting to know what the small plate with the figure 2 attached to the nearest lamp iron was for. Whilst in shops, the boiler carried by No.62437 – No.1970 which was new in October 1950 – was renumbered into the BR scheme and became No.26287. Note that N2 No.69514 is stabled behind. The Parkhead tank had been in shops from 29th March to 23rd April 1954 for an L/I but had to return for rectification (Non-Classified) on 27th April and did not depart for Glasgow until 7th May. However, that little hiccup enabled us to see – albeit at a distance – our second of the three N2s which visited the works. No.69514 was condemned sixteen months later! *R.F. Payne (ARPT).*

BR Standard Class 3 No.77017 spent all of its twelve short years at Hurlford depot working freight and passenger trains around Ayrshire but in the third week of June 1957 – it was less than three years old at the time – it ventured north-east to Inverurie works for attention. On Sunday 23rd June 1957 the 2-6-0 was pictured in the yard just north of Nos.54507 and 64547 illustrated earlier. Why the Cl.3 visited Inverurie is unknown but the Smith–Stone speedometer cable and associated connections look rather new for a device that was fitted to this locomotive when new! *C.J.B. Sanderson (ARPT).*

(*opposite*) Two more trailblazers!? (*top*) 19th August 1960 and J39 No.64897 from 52D Alnmouth arrives at Inverurie for a General overhaul which was completed 30th September 1960. It had been four years since the 0-6-0 attended works – Cowlairs then – and it looks like it hasn't been cleaned since. Yes this was No.64897's one and only visit to Inverurie. (*bottom*) On the same day J38 No.65926, in much the same external condition as the J39 is stabled in a siding at Inverurie waiting for a berth in the shops. Having arrived the day before, the Dunfermline resident was not released back into traffic until 14th October. The reason for this first visit to Inverurie was the fitting of AWS which was classified as a Casual Light repair. No.65926 would visit again, twice! *Both Howard Forster*

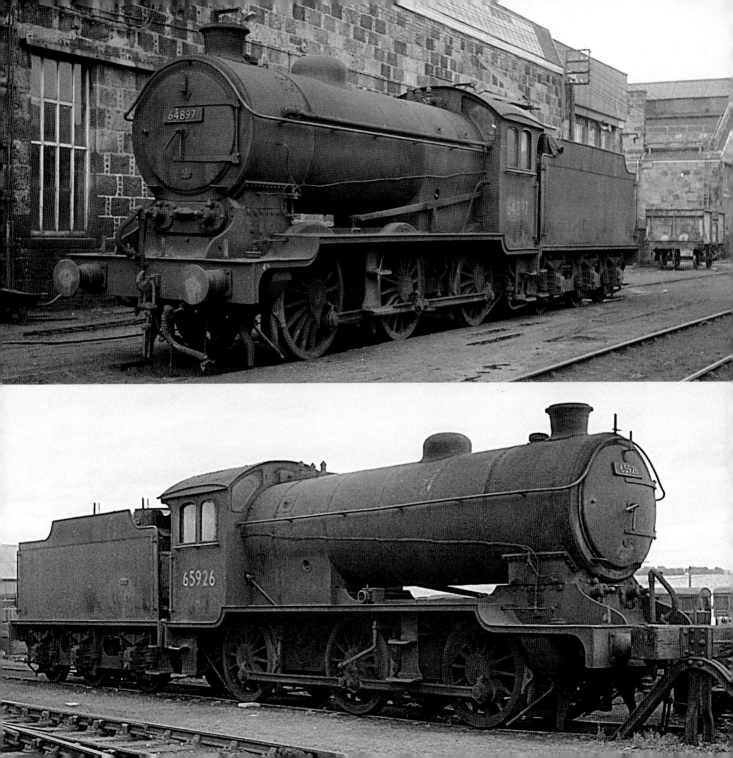

D31 No.62065 is being stripped in a seemingly haphazard way but the scrap men at Inverurie obviously knew what they were doing as they had scrapped more than twenty of this class of steam locomotives beforehand. The 4-4-0 is still attached to its tender on this 20th day of May 1949 which could be described as rather glorious unless of course you was a condemned steam locomotive. Condemned just five weeks previously on 20th April, the D31 was amongst the last of its kind with only three others Nos.62059, 62060, and 62072 outliving it and becoming Nos.62281, 62282, and 62283 respectively to release their numbers for new Peppercorn K1s. *K.H. Cockerill (ARPT).*

Between February and August 1962 (first figure) and August to October 1963 (second figure) the following types were broken up in the scrapyard:

5MT 4-6-0 0, 1; 2P 4-4-0 10, 0; 2P 0-4-4T 16, 0; 3P 4-4-0 3, 0; 2F 0-6-0 5, 0; 3F 0-6-0 6, 3; 3F 0-6-0T 2, 0; 4F 0-6-0 4, 1; J35 4, 1; J36 7, 11; J37 4, 6; J38 0, 1; J39 1, 4; J83 1, 1; J88 2, 0; K4 2, 0; N15 1, 0; V1 0, 1; V2 0, 7; V3 0, 5; WD 2-8-0 0, 4.

Z4 No.68190 and Z5 No.68192 have become the respective lasts' of their classes. Admitted there were only two representatives in each class but nevertheless for both 'lasts' to be together in the scrapyard at Inverurie works takes some coincidences falling into place. The date is Monday 13th June 1960 and the 0-4-2Ts are patiently waiting to be dealt with. Both locomotives and their erstwhile partners used to work the docks at Aberdeen but since the mid-1950s there was barely enough work for one of their kind never mind four. All four locomotives spent long periods in store taking turns to do the work which was offered. The first Z4 – 68191 – went at the end of March 1959 whereas the first Z5 – 68193 – went much earlier on 24th April 1956. It will be noted that neither of this pair got the new BR crest which is easy to understand as none of them went near works after May 1956 and the emblem was not superseded by the crest until summer 1957. All four engines had stints in private industry being loaned to distilleries especially. No.68190 had been in store at various times since March 1955 and never really recovered from those long spells out of traffic. Both engines were supplied to the GNofSR in 1915 so had put in a good stint of forty years even before storage became the norm. Condemned 28th April 1960, it would not have much longer to wait. Z5 No.68192 was also condemned on 28th April and likewise the chop was almost there! *R.F. Payne (ARPT)*.

D34 No.62467 GLENFINNAN was condemned on 10th August 1960 and by the afternoon of Monday 22nd of that month the 4-4-0 was installed in the Cemetery scrapyard at Inverurie being dismantled. This image reveals that the cutting torch has been busy around the front end releasing the boiler and smokebox from the cylinder box. Somebody has cut away the front splasher to preserve the name painted thereon; perhaps to order? One of the nameplates/splashers from GLEN MAMIE – D34 No.62482 – has been attached to the grounded van body used as a tool store on the left. That 4-4-0 had been scrapped here during the previous March. Inverurie always had a busy scrapyard with some choice locomotives spending their final days there before getting the axe. During 1961 approximately half of the output concerned thirty–six former LMS locomotives but in 1962 the number of ex–LMS engines surpassed the former LNER lot at a ratio of 60/40. In 1963 they took care of ten V2s amongst others, whilst 1964 found two A3s, three Peppercorn A1s and two more V2s were chopped before scrapping ceased. *D.R. Dunn collection. (ARPT)*.

Since 29th April 1939 B12 No.61560 – then simply 8560 – had attended Inverurie works for all its needs and overhauls. Before then, the 4-6-0 had been allocated to Great Eastern lines of the LNER and had used Stratford works for its repairs, etc. Since coming north to Scotland, No.61560 had been allocated to Kittybrewster where it had been maintained daily and looked after by shed men and engine men alike. However, on 9th May 1952 the big 4-6-0 which was by now wearing the attractive lined green livery applied at Inverurie, was condemned. Within days of that event, the B12 was moved to the scrapyard where it joined ex–Caley 2F 0-6-0 No.17380 with its LMS 31A St Rollox shedplate still in situ. The 2F had actually been withdrawn in May 1948 and for the past four years had languished at various places but mainly at Balornock shed. The opportunity to see how Inverurie could cope with what would normally be a St Rollox scrap job or even a Kilmarnock task, was taken and the ex–CR 0-6-0 was hauled up to Aberdeen and then sixteen miles beyond to what would be No.17380's final resting place. *A.R. Thompson collection (ARPT).*

KILMARNOCK

The foliage between the camera and the subject basically sum up the locomotive workshops at Kilmarnock and its immediate surroundings – tumbleweed, dereliction! However, it is 6th August 1956 and everything that can grow was growing. The locomotives in view include K2 No.61734, D40 No.62268, 4Ps Nos.40902 and 40909, and N2 69562 with a bunch of orphan tenders from previous residents which had been broken up; the tenders were sometimes returned to main works where they could be re-used but industry was interested in them too, their uses being many within steel works for instance. Locomotive repairs ceased at Kilmarnock BR workshops in 1952 and thereafter, until closure in July 1959, the shops took on the role of repairing the Scottish Region mobile crane fleet, Breakdown, Departmental, and Engineers. During the near seventy years between opening in 1856 and the end of the Glasgow & South Western Railway in 1922, Kilmarnock built some 392 steam locomotives – the first, in 1857, was a 2-2-2 Class 2 (what else?), and the last, a pair of 3F 0-6-0 tender engines which were two late examples of Hanson's 115 Class, Nos.17523 and 17524 in 1921. The works site covered some thirteen acres, the smallest in area, of all the Scottish railway locomotive workshops which became BR property. *W.S. Sellar.*

C15 No.67455 resides amongst the weeds at Kilmarnock on Saturday 18th June 1955. Already a start has been made to dismantle the Atlantic tank by removing the front buffers but little else has taken place. It appears that the LNER identity of the 4-4-2T has obviously shown through the BR applied paint but the No.67455 never had the LNER painted over, the number 67455 being the only BR identification it carried; there never was a BR emblem applied and the LNER was left untouched to its withdrawal on 11th February 1955 from Kittybrewster shed. *W.S. Sellar.*

Sister C15 No.67456 – also ex–Kittybrewster – was resident at the works on Saturday 16th October 1954. Until November 1949 the presence of former LNER locomotives terminating their operational lives at this works was an extremely rare occurrence. But from that month BR ScR started to take some – but not all – of the scrapping responsibility away from Cowlairs and Inverurie and so the likes of former North British 4-4-0s started to arrive in the first instance. These were followed by B12s from the former GNofSR lines. No less than eighteen of the C15 were broken up at Kilmarnock. *W.S. Sellar.*

Sentinel No.47182 was withdrawn from Ayr in February 1956 and was photographed at Kilmarnock on the following 10th March. The 2–cylinder chain driven shunter dates from a batch purchased by the LMS in 1930 – LMS Nos.7160–7163, makers Nos.8209–8212 – which were renumbered 7180–7183 in 1939. The allocation of this group of four 0-4-0s was diverse to say the least with 7160 going to Northampton, 7161 to Bromsgrove, 7162 to Ayr, and 7163 to Lower Darwen. By March 1944 the allocation of the group had changed in that No.7180 was at Shrewsbury, 7181 and 7183 were both at Sutton Oak, whilst 7182 remained loyal to Ayr. The end of the LMS found 7180 and 7181 had changed sheds otherwise it was all the same. To complete this short allocation history of the 'Sentinel Four' we see that 47180 did a stint at Preston in 1950 but was withdrawn from Shrewsbury in the summer of 1953. 47181 did a year at Gorton 39A off all places in 1953 but ended up at Shrewsbury via Sutton Oak and Crewe South and was withdrawn from 84G in November 1956, the longest lived of the quartet. No.47183 was withdrawn from Shrewsbury in September 1955. So, there you have it, the only LMS Sentinel to work in Scotland and the only one broken up in the country; a first for Kilmarnock! *D.R. Dunn collection (ARPT).*

Kilmarnock was responsible for cutting–up more than forty of the ex–LMS 4P 4-4-0 Compounds so beloved by Derby. On 25th May 1958 No.40920, one of Stranraer's meagre allocation, was in works for the final act which actually took place later in the summer. Over the years since these 4-4-0s had begun their one–way journeys to Kilmarnock, Stranraer has sent at least seven of her own 4P Compounds here for the chop. No.40920 was in fact the last 68C based 4P and the last of her class to be scrapped here. Note that the shedplate has been removed but a lamp has been placed on the central iron. *F.W. Hampson (ARPT).*

A line–up of four withdrawn ex–LMS 2Ps, in various states of external condition, stable in the yard at Kilmarnock works on Saturday 14th April 1962. The works had finished dismantling steam locomotives some three years before hand but the sidings set within the 13 acres became useful for storing withdrawn locomotives at a crucial time when the Scottish Region were trying to set records for locomotive withdrawals as delivery of diesel locomotives was accelerating. Of course the weather and other circumstances slowed down the slaughter of steam as the diesels struggled to cope with the winter cold and inner demons! Although a lot of withdrawn steam locomotives were put back into traffic, it didn't really affect this bunch formerly allocated to Hurlford because they were long gone. Oh yes, their numbers and withdrawal dates: Nos.40687 10/61, 40651 10/61, 40661 12/61, and 40592 12/61. *Paul Claxton.*

The line of ex-Hurlford 2Ps from another angle on 14th April 1962; the nearest tender, attached to No.40592 was No.3526, a 3500 gallon, 4–ton coal capacity tender formerly coupled to a Midland Railway 4-2-2 Single. *Paul Claxton*.

In April 1962, whilst demolition work takes place inside the old erecting shop, 2P No.40689 – withdrawn from Hurlford in October 1961 – stables undercover and away from the elements awaiting the call to a scrapyard somewhere. *Paul Claxton*.

B12 No.61502 went into Inverurie works for assessment for overhaul on 7th April 1954 but during the next couple of weeks its problems were so numerous and considerable that it was condemned on the 30th day of the month. With new BR Standard classes coming into traffic virtually daily, it was a bad time for steam locomotives older than thirty years to show anything other than normal wear and tear, defects basically meant the chop. And so it was for No.61502 from 61C Keith shed which would be replaced by a BR Standard Cl.4 2-6-4T which most enginemen took to immediately. The six-coupled tank could do anything the 4-6-0 could do but in extremes of comfort for the crews. No.61502 was taken south to Kilmarnock for breaking up and here in the works during July 1954 it was still looking fairly decent externally. The former Great Eastern express passenger locomotive had arrived in Scotland at Kittybrewster on 8th April 1931 when it was just shy of twenty years old. During that time up to withdrawal, it had worked mainly over the GNofSR area serving at Elgin and Keith sheds besides Kittybrewster; it even did a stint at Eastfield from November 1942 to June 1943. However, the Stratford built engine had paid its way time and again; the final act was to recoup value from its scrap metal and it was now in the right place for that deed to be enacted. Although still wearing its 61C shedplate nearly four months after withdrawal, note the legend **K BREWSTER** annotation on the bufferbeam. No.61502 hadn't been allocated to Kittybrewster since 11th December 1943. Still they are fairly laid-back in NE Scotland! *K.H. Cockerill (ARPT).*

Another aspect of the B12's predicament! It appears that the tender has just been emptied of coal. Now where were those coupling rods? Very visible in this view of the building is the division between the original stone-walled workshops and the brick-built extension. Besides these 4-6-0s handled by Kilmarnock, it must be recorded that most of the former Caledonian 4P 4-6-0s which entered BR ownership were cut-up here shortly after Nationalisation. The Heath Robinson overhead plumbing is typical of the makeshift instances found around industrial installations pre-H&SE! Now where has that path gone! *K.H. Cockerill (ARPT).*

By Sunday 25th May 1958 when this scene was recorded outside the former erecting shop at Kilmarnock, the D30 class were being decimated with less than half of them still intact. No.62434 KETTLEDRUMMLE had succumbed on 24th April at Dundee shed and had arrived here during May complete with all its various plates but minus that front screw coupling. The 4-4-0 was removed from this position and located at the side of the shops but it remained intact throughout the summer of 1958 until eventually dealt with as the nights grew longer. On the right, mounted on a bogie well wagon, is an intact boiler and a firebox which were no doubt bound to one of the many scrapyards found in the central belt of Scotland and which were biding their time before BR started selling whole locomotives and the likes of Kilmarnock's time as a locomotive scrapyard was ended. *F.W. Hampson (ARPT).*

'Small Ben' No.14397 BEN-Y-GLOE languishes at Kilmarnock on Friday 20th May 1949. Not having acquired its BR number, No.14397 was withdrawn from Inverness in January 1949 and eventually hauled south to this place for scrapping. Even then Kilmarnock was dealing with all the withdrawn locomotives formerly handed at Lochgorm, and also some of the overflow from Cowlairs, Inverurie and St Rollox. Between a visit to Kilmarnock on 2nd May before the arrival of this locomotive, and 14th August 1949, the 'Small Ben' appears to have been, greeted, photographed, sorted, and cut-up as not a trace remained by the latter date. It appears that the scrapping process was carried out in 'fits and starts' at Kilmarnock with no regular pattern of locomotives entering the works and being scrapped. For instance 1950 was a year in which few locomotives were dealt with whilst at the same time overhauls and repairs remained constant. *K.H. Cockerill (ARPT).*

The works shunter on Sunday 9th June 1957 was one of the ex–Caley 'Pugs' No.56028 which had latterly been allocated to Greenock Ladyburn shed, or so its appeared! In actuality the little 0-4-0ST had been withdrawn from Ladyburn earlier in the week and was quickly dispatched to Kilmarnock for processing. The works here had broken up quite a few of the former North British 'Pug' Y9s but not too many of these somewhat rarer former CR four-coupled saddletanks. Again, this was another class which had not arrived into the BR era in great numbers with only fourteen of the original thirty–nine having survived the twenty–five years of LMS stewardship. However, BR like the LMS beforehand had utilised those 0-4-0STs far and wide with examples working in Bromsgrove, Burton-on-Trent, Corkerhill, Crewe works, Dawsholm, Greenock, Inverness, Kipps, Motherwell, Preston, Shrewsbury, St Margarets, St Rollox works, and Yoker; the fact that fourteen locations are listed is pure coincidence! Note that our subject has kept that lovely tall original chimney. *W.S. Sellar.*

D40 No.62268 alongside the shops on 6th August 1956. The 4-4-0 had made the long trek from Keith to get here although the chances are it travelled via Inverurie who signed it off; the worksplate has gone but the 61C shed plate and front numberplate are still in situ; the age of railwayana popularity was still in its infancy! One of the unnamed members of D40 class, No.62268 was one of eight of her kind sent to Kilmarnock for breaking up. Six of them came in 1955 and the last one, No.62264 arrived in August 1957, again, from Keith. *W.S. Sellar.*

F4 No.67157 was the only one of her class to be cut–up at Kilmarnock, a deed which took place shortly after August 1956. The 2-4-2T was transferred to Scotland on 25th January 1948 being allocated to 61A Kittybrewster as a late replacement for one of the three F4s which were transferred to the Scottish area of the LNER in 1931 – Nos.7176, condemned April 1943, 7222 (67164) condemned 27th August 1951, and 7236 (67151) condemned 28th August 1951. On arrival in Scotland a cowcatcher had been fitted at Inverurie in February 1948 but that had been removed at withdrawal – 8th June 1956 – before the F4 was sent to Kilmarnock. The devices were then fitted to Ivatt Cl.2 No.46460 – both ends – which had taken over the St Combs light railway duties working from Fraserburgh shed. Oh yes, the passing of this particular engine at Kilmarnock saw Class F4 become extinct! *W.S. Sellar.*

Waiting for the New Year festivities to subside, Drummond 2F 'Jumbo' No.57315 stands outside the erecting shop on 2nd January 1956 having been parted from its tender in the previous year. The 0-6-0 had spent most of its BR life working from Ayr shed and was withdrawn from there in December 1955; indeed, most of its LMS lifetime was also performed from Ayr too. Some 244 locomotives comprised this class which entered traffic between 1883 and 1897. The first withdrawal took place in 1946 when they were all a bit 'long-in-the tooth' but some 238 managed to become BR property. No.57315 ceased to exist shortly after work resumed with the ending of the New Year break. *W.S. Sellar.*

The date is 5th November 1955 and ex–LMS 2P No.40686 from 67B Hurlford has not come to Kilmarnock for breaking up, nor has it come to celebrate Guy Fawkes Night with the resident workforce. It has come to exchange tenders because its own tender must have had a major defect. Anyway at this time Kilmarnock was breaking up the ex-LMS and Midland 4P Compounds and many of their tenders were worth keeping for such eventualities as this. No.40686 went back into traffic – hopefully having had the new tender cleaned – and worked for another five years or so before being withdrawn in October 1961. The 4-4-0 was eventually cut up at the Heatheryknowe C&W works. Note the discarded buffer on the ground! *W.S. Sellar.*

Under BR control the works continued repairing locomotives until 1952 but a visit four years beforehand, shortly after Nationalisation, on Tuesday 26th October 1948 found the following locomotives present and being attended to, their home shed is recorded alongside:

4P 4-4-0	—	41133 Ayr.
4MT 2-6-4T	—	42419 Greenock.
5MT 2-6-0	—	2757 Kingmoor, 42803 Kingmoor, 42907 Kingmoor, 42927 Ayr.
4F 0-6-0	—	3973 Kingmoor.
3P 4-4-0	—	14497 Greenock.
2P 0-4-4T	—	55125 Motherwell.
4P 4-6-2T	—	55360 Beattock.
2F 0-6-0	—	17256 Motherwell, 17325 Motherwell, 17443 Polmadie.
3F 0-6-0	—	57557 St Rollox.

The scrap yard contained the following which were all withdrawn:

3F 0-6-0T	—	16270 Motherwell.
2F 0-6-0	—	17421 Stranraer, 17471 Dawsholm.
3F 0-6-0	—	17606 Motherwell.

During November 1949 the following entered the shops for overhaul:

2P 4-4-0	—	40638 Ayr, 661 Hurlford.
3P 4-4-0	—	54492 Greenock Ladyburn.
4P 4-4-0	—	1141 Kingmoor.
3P 2-6-2T	—	40152 Dawsholm.
4P 2-6-4T	—	42164 Hamilton.
5F 2-6-0	—	42905 Kingmoor.
2F 0-6-0	—	57264 Stirling, 57353 Hurlford, 17359 Corkerhill.
3F 0-6-0	—	57625 Polmadie.
4F 0-6-0	—	4329 Corkerhill.
3F 0-6-0T	—	56314 Polmadie, 56375 Grangemouth.
5MT 4-6-0	—	45086 Perth.
2P 0-4-4T	—	55201 Polmadie, 55225 Corkerhill, 55265 Polmadie.

On Thursday 10th November 1949 three ex–LNER locomotives withdrawn during the previous September and officially recorded as cut up at Cowlairs, had arrived at Kilmarnock for scrapping thus:

D1 4-4-0	—	2214 Hawick.
D33 4-4-0	—	2458 Bathgate.
D34 4-4-0	—	2481 GLEN OGLE Eastfield.

On Tuesday 8th January 1952 the following were being dealt with in the Erecting shop:

2P 4-4-0	—	40670 Ayr.
3P 2-6-2T	—	40151 Hamilton.
5MT 2-6-0	—	42744 Hurlford.
2F 0-6-0	—	57236 Hurlford.

The scrap yard which had been continuously receiving consignments from Cowlairs, Inverurie, Lochgorm and St Rollox was less busy with just two locomotives resident but it was about to start receiving locomotives from far and wide:

4P 4-6-0	—	54648 Hamilton.
2F 0-6-0	—	57344 Dumfries.

From the cessation of locomotive repairs and overhauls in 1952 to closure in 1959 the workshops concentrated on plant – mobile cranes – repair and overhaul but managed at the same time to scrap more than one hundred and sixty steam locomotives in that period. Taking one year – 1956 – as a typical twelve–month period, we list the following withdrawn locomotives which entered the scrap yard. The list is not definitive because remnants of the previous years' intake were still intact and the old adage about missing the odd one – or two – still stood:

4P 4-4-0	—	40902 Dumfries, 40908 Corkerhill, 40909 Corkerhill, 40915 Hurlford, 40938 Perth, 41131 Stranraer, 41177 Stranraer.
Sentinel 0-4-0T	—	47182 Ayr.
2P 0-4-4T	—	55162 Inverness.
3F 0-6-0T	—	56231 Kingmoor, 56317 Kingmoor, 56319 Hamilton.
2F 0-6-0	—	57230 Polmadie, 57315 Ayr, 57412 Polmadie, 57456 Dawsholm.
D40 4-4-0	—	62268 Keith.
K2 2-6-0	—	61720 Boston, 61727 Immingham, 61734 Keith.
C15 4-4-2T	—	67459 Polmont, 67463 Polmont, 67466 Dunfermline, 67478 Keith, 67480 Eastfield.
C16 4-4-2T	—	67483 Dundee Tay Bridge, 67493 Thornton Jct., 67495 Hawick, 67498 Dundee TB, 67499 Dundee TB.
F4 2-4-2T	—	67157 Kittybrewster.
N2 0-6-2T	—	69562 Parkhead.
Q1 0-8-0T	—	69927 Eastfield.

LOCHGORM

The former Highland Railway locomotive works at Inverness Lochgorm lost their importance at Grouping, the LMS realising that they had an embarrassment of assets in Scotland and that one workshop – St Rollox – could cope with heavy overhauls whilst Lochgorm and Kilmarnock could be regarded as downgraded to Intermediate level workshops where boiler changes would not be carried out or even lifted from the frames. Of course it took a few years after 1923 before the radical changes necessary could be implemented but as withdrawals of the more ancient pre–Grouping types accelerated then the requirement to shop them diminished. When the last General overhaul was performed at Lochgorm is unknown by this compiler but by 1930 St Rollox was taking in many of the ex–HR engines for Generals whilst Lochgorm was performing Light Intermediate overhauls and anything below that classification. The picture above shows what Lochgorm was doing in the 1950s with four Stanier Class 5s and their tenders filling one road of the Erecting shop whilst all the necessary equipment, spares and tools to work on them was stacked over the space taken up by the other two roads in the shop. You can see the type of overhaul taking place with axleboxes, bearings, cylinders, smokeboxes and minor boiler work being performed. This image is undated but the locomotives present were all assembled in Lochgorm shops in March 1956 so we can take that month as our approximate date. It will be noticed that all of the '5s' were fitted with tablet–catchers so they we all 'local.' This useful outstation in the Highlands closed in 1959 to steam locomotives but was then adapted to tend to the new diesel motive power which required much more refinement and certainly more sanitized conditions. *J.D. Mills, M. Halbert collection.*

Same shop, different day and a change of customers: the date is 3rd August 1956, a Friday, and in the shop now are Class 5s Nos.45443, 45081, 45162, and three ex–Caledonian 3P 4-4-0s Nos.54466, 54484, and 54496. The far end of the workspace is being utilised more and two roads are now in use. The same applied at this end where the centre road is given over to the storage and work on wheelsets. For those of you who have noticed the different roof trussing, and cladding, there is a vast difference between the roof above the nearest locomotive where tie-bars are used, and the rest of the shop where timber beams, in conjunction with tie-bars are used. The glazing set into the roof is also different in the two sections; and why was the crane rail painted white along much of the shop yet a darker colour has been applied nearer the camera? *F.W. Hampson (ARPT).*

(opposite page) **Stripped of its dignity and much else,** the former HR 0-4-4T No.55053 rests on blocks in the Erecting shop at Lochgorm in August 1957 some seven months after it was withdrawn. Built at Lochgorm in 1906, as HR No.45, the little tank was one of four built to work in pairs on the Lybster and the Dornoch branches; No.55053 was not only the last survivor of that quartet but she was also the final operational ex–HR locomotive. This engine was the only HR locomotive to receive full lining on black livery – note the lining around the front spectacle plate. However, an axle failure whilst working on the Dornoch line in January 1957 brought an early demise for this 0-4-4T when it should probably have had a couple of years in service which would possibly have taken it to the closure of the Dornoch branch. *D. Fairley (ARPT).*

Another one which got away! Highland 'Ben' 2P No.54398 BEN ALDER the last of the class was kept in open storage at Lochgorm circa 1954 but none of the usual chimney covering exercise had taken place nor had any of the motion been greased. Withdrawn in February 1953, the 4-4-0 was the subject of talk and rumour about possible preservation and for a long time it was thought that BR would actually take responsibility for the 4-4-0 and restore it to Highland livery. Built in July 1898 by Dubs & Co., as HR No.2, it was not even a Lochgorm build unlike the nine built during 1899–1900 at Inverness – Nos.9 to 17 – but they had all been withdrawn by April 1950 and somebody was looking for a suitable candidate and came up with BEN ALDER just in the nick of time. Alas, No.54398 was scrapped in 1967 but not before being taken to various locations in the Scottish Region for storage; Boat of Garten was one site where the engine shed was later demolished so requiring another building near Glasgow to be used. However each move south took the 4-4-0 nearer to the scrapyards of the industrial belt which were gobbling up everything BR during that fateful decade which saw the demise of virtually everything steam. In the National Archive at Kew there is a reference to No.54398 thus: *AN 111/606 described as Historical relics: Highland Railway steam locomotive no 2 'Ben Alder', date 1965 Oct 1 - 1966 Jan 31. Former reference in its original department 24-7-12. Closure status: Open Document, Open description.* The rumours, it turns out, were not! So, which nameless Richard Cranium gave the order to send the 4-4-0 to the scrapyard? *R.F. Payne (ARPT).*

ST ROLLOX

St Rollox locomotive workshop was created by the Caledonian Railway and opened in 1854 to build, repair and dispose of locomotives of the CR fleet. Extension of the various shops had taken place over the decades before Grouping mainly in 1870 and the years of plenty around 1884 when all the railways of Britain appeared to be experiencing a boom with industrial output expanding. The building of locomotives ceased at St Rollox in 1928 after LMS Standard 0-6-0 4F tender engine No.4476 was put into traffic. From there onwards it was all repairs with the works looking after the LMS fleet in Scotland (Northern Division) except for the Pacifics based at Polmadie but including the whole of Kingmoor's allocation too. By 1960 St Rollox was taking on more former LMS types and less ex–Caley types through natural wastage. BR Standards were also occasional visitors but the Scottish Region main-line diesel locomotive fleet became the main emphasis with heavy repairs and overhauls becoming the new regime. Steam locomotives were 'redirected' to Cowlairs whilst the former Caley workshops underwent a modernisation refit to help it cope with the growing diesel fleet.

At any one time from April 1960 the locomotives visiting for overhaul consisted mainly of LMS types with a few pre-Group designs and 'others' thus: CR 2F 0-6-0 2; CR 3F 0-6-0T 1; CR 3F 0-6-0 1; LMS 3P 2-6-2T 2; LMS 4P 2-6-4T 3; LMS 5F 2-6-0 2; LMS 5MT 4-6-0 17; LMS Cl.6P 2; BR Cl.5 4-6-0 1; BR Cl.4 2-6-4T 1; Type 2 ML Diesel 1; 0-6-0 DE Shunter 2.

Fifteen months later in June 1961 the situation had changed in favour of the diesels but steam was still being catered for thus: CR 2F 0-6-0 1; CR 3F 0-6-0 2; LMS 4P 2-6-4T 4; LMS 5F 2-6-0 3; LMS 5MT 13; LMS 6P 4-6-0 3; Type 2 ML Diesel 7; 0-6-0 DE Shunter 4.

St Rollox works shunter on 9th June 1957, 0F 0-4-0ST No.56025 which had spent a long time doing this job and would see the duty through to the end. *W.S. Sellar.*

So that's how it was done! A painter applies the number transfers to the cabside of this ex-Caley 3P 4-4-0 on Monday 21st May 1956. The lining has all been achieved using chalk, a straight edge, a loaded paint brush and a steady hand but to speed things up, not to mention standardising the size of these figures. Transfers for numbers were adopted throughout BR once the corporate font had been finalised circa 1949. No.54500 was Perth based throughout its BR lifetime and during the war years of the LMS period too. The 3P was withdrawn from 63A in March 1962. *F.W. Hampson (ARPT).*

Early start! No.54500 before the lining was applied. 'Man with chalk' and a very steady hand, not to mention decades of experience uses the chalk on this fine morning to show the painters where to apply those different colours for the lining. He has already tackled the tender and somebody is getting that lot on the way now. The splasher will take a little time but there is a method and he knows it inside-out! This covered area of the yard must have been an outside annexe to the Paint shop and was especially useful during the summer months and rainy days to complete jobs. The 4-4-0 looks even better from this aspect. Now, I wonder what kind of time allowance was given for the painters and sign-writers to complete their task on a 3P 4-4-0 for instance? *See* also page 22. *F.W. Hampson (ARPT)*.

Just across the yard from the painters during that same morning in May 1956, the works pilot stands awaiting the next job whilst a bricklayer – one of BR's own no doubt attached to this workshop – checks his levels. A couple of the yard personnel look on at the builders' handiwork as all around them things need to be done or are being done. The number of trades working in a works like St Rollox was many indeed; some of the obvious examples associated with locomotive care would be fitters, boiler–smiths, coppersmiths, etc. but bricklayers, plumbers, and other maintenance trades were required to keep the buildings going year after year. Amongst the locomotives requiring attention on this day are BR Standard Cl.4 2-6-4T No.80129 which was new during the previous December and had spent the last six months working extensively from Polmadie, without so much as a rag being drawn across its bodywork. Stanier Cl.5 No.45008 was completing a major overhaul and had yet to get its cab roof back from the Fabrication shop not to mention the firebox covering too. An unidentified ex–LMS Compound 4P 4-4-0 was in the yard as was 3F 0-6-0 No.57620 from Forres; three years hence and the 60E goods engine would transfer to Polmadie. *F.W. Hampson (ARPT).*

Saturday 21st May 1949 with a selection of locomotives being got ready for steaming whilst still under the care of the painters! Note there is quite a lot of smoke beneath the canopy which will not be doing a great deal of good to the paint schemes. 'Beetle-crusher' No.56167 from Polmadie wears the BRITISH RAILWAYS interim insignia used prior to the introduction of the BR emblem. The letters and figures at this period were all applied using the sign-writers skills as the transfer sizes and the font were yet to be totally agreed and then standardised. One of Kingmoor's Stanier Cl.5s, No.44902 stands behind the 2F 0-6-0T. *K.H. Cockerill (ARPT).*

We have no date for this image of 2FT No.56335 outside the Erecting shop during an early afternoon of what appears to be a Sunday. The six-coupled tank was allocated to Motherwell until October 1957 but then transferred to Polmadie where it worked until withdrawn in July 1960. Looking at No.56335 here it is obvious that there was much to be done before she was released back into traffic wherever that may have been. *A.R. Thompson collection (ARPT).*

Here's one that was finished earlier and what an ex–works former Caledonian Railway 3F 0-6-0T should look like. No.56255 was all but ready for steaming and testing before returning home to Hamilton. The soot stains on the brickwork above the doorways was caused not only by the works pilot, which had a tendency to encroach just inside the threshold of the shops in order to extract whatever locomotive was exiting the shops after overhaul, but also locomotives being steam tested that may have required rectification or such like. *C.J.B. Sanderson (ARPT).*

It wasn't every day that Royalty visited St Rollox and 'Princess Royal' No.46200 THE PRINCESS ROYAL spent one day – or some hours of that day – at the works on 10th September 1950 for what was recorded as a Light Casual repair. The reason for the visit can be seen at the rear of the Pacific where a couple of personnel with oxy-acetylene gear are welding a patch onto the bottom rear corner of the tender side. This indicated that either the tender had a leak, or it had been damaged in a minor collision as was an everyday occurrence on BR. At the time No.46200 was a Crewe North engine and Polmadie must have sent her across to St Rollox for attention. Note that she is in steam so made her own way there and back between works and shed. It was obviously not an everyday event either having a Pacific visit as the management appear to have shown up to watch proceedings which must have been around lunchtime or just beforehand. You can imagine the telephone call from the Shedmaster at 66A to the Works Manager at St Rollox asking a favour to get the big engine back into traffic with minimum fuss. Sometimes such hasty repairs were carried out on shed but Polmadie either had no suitable plate, paint, or fitter available? No.46200 went into works at Crewe on 14th December 1959 and emerged on 30th January after a Heavy General with the same tender – No.9376 – attached. It was its final shopping's prior to withdrawal during week ending 17th November 1962. As though to prove a point about keeping locomotives in traffic rather than taking then out for minor repairs, 1959 turned out to be the Pacific's most productive year of the decade – not including 1950 – with 58,998 revenue miles completed. The date in question was in fact a Sunday so many of the personnel in the picture might have been brought in especially or were already in work doing some overtime. Now, how many enthusiasts witnessed this event? Finally, all repairs and overhauls carried out on 'Princess Royal' class engines were done at Crewe but two instances bucked that trend; from 13th November 1951 to 17th March 1952 No.46203 attended the works at Derby where it was given a Heavy Intermediate. And the event described above was the second instance where a works other than Crewe dealt with a 'Princess Royal' *Ian Falcus*.

St Rollox works yard on a glorious Sunday 25th January 1953 with the pile of scrap in the left foreground giving a clue as to what was the main activity in this section of the premises. Ex–CR 2F No.57410, formerly of Hamilton shed, languishes centre–stage awaiting a fate from which there would be no escape. Although the cab of the 0-6-0 displays a painted symbol denoting that it is withdrawn, the official withdrawal of this locomotive did not take place until Thursday 12th February 1953, some eighteen days hence! When eventually the deed was carried out, No.57410 was destined for a trip to Kilmarnock where she would be dismantled and certain components returned to St Rollox for either re-use or sale to an outside agency. Surrounding the 2F are boilers which had been sent back from Kilmarnock. Immediately behind are a couple of Fowler tenders which up to December last had been coupled to Scottish based ex–LMS Compound 4P 4-4-0s of which six had recently been speedily dealt with at Kilmarnock – Nos.40911, 40918, 40922, 41109, 41171, and 41182. The scrap pile by-the-way contains the metallic remains of locomotives, carriages and wagons which had been scrapped by St Rollox at some time before Kilmarnock was designated as the scrapping works for the Scottish Region. *W.S. Sellar.*

(above) It wasn't all locomotives at St Rollox! Adjacent to the Locomotive shops was the carriage works where vehicles such as this former Pullman could be seen undergoing overhaul. This specimen is SC216M which as can be seen was a Restaurant Car working over what route? If anyone can enlighten this compiler who does not know too much about carriage workings he would be most grateful. The wooden panelling below the windows can be just made out otherwise the carriage is in the lined BR maroon livery of the period. The date is 15th December 1959, a particularly sunny one note. *(below)* Another Restaurant Car, this one a twelve–wheel job numbered SC21X and photographed on 18th April 1955. Is that the early BR 'blood-and-custard' livery? Up until the creation of the wagon works at Barassie, St Rollox used to handle wagons too. *Both W.S. Sellar.*

That 0F again! This time the 'Pug' waits outside the Erecting shop main entrance on 9th June 1957. Certain parts of the locomotives' superstructure have been cleaned and even bulled-up whereas below the running plate the frames, wheels and motion have been neglected but this engine was never seen by the general public anyway and those enthusiasts visiting the works would understand! Now, the eagle-eyed amongst you will have noticed the 16-ton mineral wagon behind the saddletank; the little engine just about manages to hide most of the vehicle giving us a reminder of how small these four-coupled tanks actually were. *F.W. Hampson (ARPT)*.

A rainy 27th July 1965 and the works yard is looking somewhat derelict as the transition from steam to diesel locomotive overhauls is still taking place. Steam is long gone but the detritus of their presence here is still in evidence. The solitary steam occupant is a former Glasgow & South Western '322' Class 0-6-0T which had been working in private industry but had returned to the fold looking somewhat neglected. Although it doesn't appear to be anything special in this image, the 0-6-0T was quite precious in that it was the only surviving G&SWR steam locomotive. Its pre-Group number was No.324 and it was one of three built in 1917 and which later passed into LMS ownership becoming their No.16379. The engine, along with sister No.16378 was sold out of service in 1934 – the final member of the trio No.16377 had been withdrawn in 1932 and scrapped! No.16378 went to Hatfield Main Colliery in South Yorkshire and put in many years of service before it too was scrapped. No.16379 also went to a coal mine, Hafod Colliery in Denbigh where it was working up to the early 1960s but was placed into store with a view to selling for scrap. In 1964 somebody within BR realised – hopefully there was some panic accompanying the realisation – that the only remaining G&SWR locomotive was in fact that hulk at Hafod. BR quickly acquired the unidentified six–coupled wreck and had it taken to Glasgow where it ended up at St Rollox, the former LMS workshop. What happened afterwards is now history but this less than perfect but historically important image gives you an idea of what happened purely by chance to what was the only G&SW locomotive in existence at the end of steam. *N.W. Skinner (ARPT).*

A section of the Erecting shop at St Rollox in July 1960 with ex–LMS Standard types dominating; besides the five Class 5s, a 'Crab' is near the camera whilst 'Jubilee' No.45714 REVENGE is made ready for painting after having gone through a Heavy Intermediate overhaul – 28th June to 6th August 1960 – its last visit to a main works before withdrawal in July 1963. The Kingmoor based 4-6-0 was one of those Jubilees which were always coupled to a Fowler tender. When new in July 1936, it was initially coupled to tender No.3911 which was from 'Royal Scot' No.6124 and was already nine years old! No.45714 was coupled to three other Fowler tenders during its life but in August 1951 it met up again with No.3911 and remained coupled for the rest of its life! *Stuart Ashworth collection.*

In a corner of the Erecting shop, seemingly out of the way, the preserved ex–Highland Railway Jones Goods No.103 is stored up on blocks, clear of any rails, on an unknown date but post May 1956. Where the tender was at this time is also unknown but the Tender shop would be a serious assumption; its wheels were probably also clear of rails, on blocks. Between this date and its eventual retirement in a museum, this 4–6–0 would do some travelling around the country hauling enthusiasts' specials and even getting involved in a feature film about early aviators. Withdrawn in 1934 as LMS No.17916, aged forty years, the 4F was preserved initially in green livery as here and renumbered to its former HR number 103. The 4-6-0 had been gathering dust inside the Paint shop here on 21st May 1949 but had obviously been moved to a more convenient location. In 1959 it was restored to working order and repainted in a Stroudley yellow livery and then the fun started. *E.E. Smith*.